PANDA CUBS

JEN BESEL

BLACK RABBIT BOOKS

Bolt Jr. is published by Black Rabbit Books
P.O. Box 227, Mankato, Minnesota, 56002.
www.blackrabbitbooks.com

Michael Sellner, designer; Omay Ayres, photo researcher

Names: Besel, Jennifer M., author.
Title: Panda cubs / by Jen Besel.
Description: Mankato, Minnesota : Black Rabbit Books, [2020] | Series: Bolt Jr. baby animals | Includes bibliographical references and index. |Audience: Age 6-8. | Audience: K to Grade 3.
Identifiers: LCCN 2018059386 (print) | LCCN 2018061581 (ebook) | ISBN 9781623101473 (ebook) | ISBN 9781623101411 (library binding) | ISBN 9781644660973 (paperback)
Subjects: LCSH: Pandas—Infancy—Juvenile literature.
Classification: LCC QL737.C27 (ebook) | LCC QL737.C27 B4546 2020 (print) | DDC 599.78913/92—dc23
LC record available at https://lccn.loc.gov/2018059386

Image Credits

Alamy: Xinhua, 6–7; Getty: AFP, 23; Gary Vestal, Cover; Keren Su, 20–21; iStock: Foreverhappy-Mee, 5; Shutterstock: Alesikka, 3, 24; Ecaterina Sciuchina, 15 (panda); Eric Isselee, 4, 8–9, 10, 13, 21 (inset); Gang Liu, 16–17; Hung Chung Chih, 10–11; Larisska_c, 14 (panda); Maks Narodenko, 7 (ball); noraismail, 1; Ondrej Prosicky, 18; Peter Gudella, 12; Pyty, 14–15 (map)

Contents

CHAPTER 1

A Hungry Baby

A baby giant panda leaves the **den**. It walks to its mother. But the cub's legs are still **wobbly**. The baby trips over a branch. But it gets back up. The cub needs its mother. The baby is hungry!

den: the home of some kinds of wild animals

wobbly: not steady

WEIGHT COMPARISON

newborn cub

3 to 5 ounces
(85 to 142 grams)

Growing Fast

Newborn cubs are helpless. They don't have fur either. Their mothers care for them. Mothers don't even leave them to eat! But cubs grow quickly. They'll get their fur in about three weeks. In three months, they can crawl around.

baseball
5.25 ounces
(149 grams)

PARTS OF A
Panda Cub

fur
ears
eyes
mouth

CHAPTER 2

Food and Homes

Panda cubs eat a lot! At first, they drink their mothers' milk. As they grow, cubs begin eating **bamboo**. Cubs don't know which bamboo to eat. Mother pandas teach them.

bamboo: a kind of plant

FACT

Pandas eat bamboo stems and leaves.

A Forest Home

Giant pandas only live in China. They live in mountain forests. The forests are cool and wet. Mothers make homes in **hollow** trees. They climb high up the mountains. There's good food there.

hollow: having an unfilled space

Giant Panda Range

China
KEY
= where giant pandas live

CHAPTER 3

Growing Up

Cubs have a lot to learn. Mother pandas are their teachers. They show cubs what to eat. They show them how to get around. And they even show them how to play.

FACT

Cubs copy their mothers' actions.

Making Their Own Homes

Baby pandas don't stay with their mothers forever. They leave when they're about two years old. They make new homes.

Cubs are all grown by their fourth birthdays. They soon have cubs of their own.

300

Adult Panda's Weight

up to 300 pounds
(136 kilograms)

Bonus Facts

Cubs play in the snow.

Only about **1,800** pandas are left in the world.

Adult pandas eat for 12 hours a day.

Pandas live up to 20 years in the wild.

wild: not living in a house or zoo

READ MORE/WEBSITES

Boothroyd, Jennifer. *From Cub to Panda*. Start to Finish. Minneapolis: Lerner Publications, 2017.

Manushkin, Fran. *Bamboo for Me, Bamboo for You!* New York: Aladdin, 2017.

Trueit, Trudi Strain. *Giant Pandas*. Wild Bears. Mankato, MN: Amicus High Interest/Amicus Ink, 2016.

Giant Panda
kids.nationalgeographic.com/animals/giant-panda/#giant-panda-eating.jpg

Giant Panda
kids.sandiegozoo.org/animals/giant-panda

Giant Panda
nationalzoo.si.edu/animals/giant-panda

GLOSSARY

bamboo (bam-BOO)—a kind of plant

den (DEN)—the home of some kinds of wild animals

hollow (HAH-low)—having an unfilled space

wild (WIHLD)—not living in a house or zoo

wobbly (WAH-blee)—not steady

INDEX